A Walk to Passchendaele

A Walk to Passchendaele

Julian Nicholls

The Pentland Press Limited
Edinburgh · Cambridge · Durham · USA

© Julian Nicholls

First published in 1997
by The Pentland Press Limited
1 Hutton Close
South Church
Bishop Auckland
Co. Durham

ISBN: 1 85821 523 4

Typeset by George Wishart & Associates, Whitley Bay
Printed and bound by Antony Rowe Ltd., Chippenham

*Dedicated to
the young men of
both sides who never
came home.*

Those who went

They say that Flanders fields are red
Where lie the young, who now are dead,
Who came in hope, to die in fear,
The poppies tell us every year.

Amidst this land of deep despair
The scent of death hangs in the air.
Why! They call from graves below
Was it all just a show?

Mothers cry for sons no more
Last kissed before they went to war,
Fine boys were they, who said goodbye,
Be home in June, who knows, July.

In English meadows maidens weep
For cherished ones, now at sleep,
Remembering only youth and verve
Blinded by the will to serve.

Julian Nicholls

Introduction

After much soul-searching and spurred on by an avid interest in all that took part in Flanders in 1917 I decided to visit Ypres. My main purpose was to analyse certain contributory aspects concerning the offensive of July–November 1917. Like so many before me I had been gutsily fed on information from the numerous writings and archive wealth regarding this brutal confrontation. However, during the process of my studies I came to rely a great deal on my own vivid imagination, but this was not enough. For what I had to do was quite simple... I would visit Flanders and attempt the difficult task of transcribing the mind's pictures into some form of reality in the locality and confines of where it had all taken place originally.

So, on a beautiful July day in 1994 and blessed with exceptionally better weather than our 1917 contemporaries, my wife and I set out on foot on what I came to regard as a personal pilgrimage of respect to all those brave young men who had failed to return to 'Blighty' and home.

My journey was to be straightforward and I had decided previously that if chronicled, my work would be simple and devoid of all complications.

On most occasions I was accompanied by my wife Jeanne,

who, through it all would become a 'born again' walker. We visited many cemeteries and battle fields culminating on the final day in walking the 'Ridge' from Tyne-Cot cemetery into Passchendaele itself.

Along the way we were traversing one of the largest killing fields in the history of European warfare and at the end of our walk we retired to take coffee in a local estaminet. Had this been seventy-six years previously we would have sat amongst ruins and no doubt for company would have had numerous corpses of those who fell here.

For me, days would come and go but none would be so moving as then, as I pictured all that had taken place.

To future pilgrims may I say what a moving experience it is, but then again so it should be.

'Lest we forget'.

Preface

For many years the name Passchendaele possessed a remote connection to something that had taken place during World War One. In the course of reading world warfare over the years this mystical name would never fail from time to time to appear as if to say, 'Read about me! Find out what happened here.' This in itself instilled in me an almost obsessive urge to gain greater knowledge. I was being enticed by a mysterious lady to whom I succumbed wholeheartedly in order that I might at last discover and attempt to understand what took place in 1917 near to this village in the heartland of rural Belgium.

What I was about to discover was the magnitude of the slaughter, the ultimate sacrifice of tens of thousands of humans whose presence in this place at the same time, and also, for what was considered the same purpose, was solely defined by the mere difference in uniform and language.

I would be left forever with the knowledge of the extremes man would aspire to regarding the infliction of pain, suffering and death upon his fellow man.

I would almost taste the mud of Flanders fields as I tried to understand, often tearfully, the carnage that took place in the degrading filth of what would be ever remembered as the Battle of Passchendaele.

Its registration in the annals of military history was due entirely to its geographical location, this once sleepy rural Belgian village whose original inhabitants would often stare at the distant Ypres across the lowland from the elevated ridge on which their village stood. Yet they as inhabitants of this hamlet could never perceive how this elevation above the surrounding countryside would be the reason for the most futile confrontation of two enemy forces ever.

With regard to the First World War this would be the 'killing field' of all killing fields. A place where one, if not killed by bullet or shell, would suffer death through disease caused by festering wounds. In many cases severely wounded would disappear in the water filled shell holes, to be remembered only by the often used line 'known only unto God'.

Casualty figures can only be estimated and I would emphasise the world estimate. During the three month battle, 31 July to 12 November, until Passchendaele was finally taken, the cost in human terms was approximately 300,000 British, 250,000 Germans and 9,000 French. There were also others from the various allies.

Sadly, there would never be precise documentation but it must be reasonably safe to assume that the total casualty figure would exceed half a million killed and wounded from both adversaries in what had become a war of attrition.

Perhaps another realistic estimate would have been achieved by simply counting the troops who went forth compared to those who survived. Total accuracy would in no way be achieved but it would serve in a small way to confirm the cost to humanity.

And for what purpose? Peoples around the world have asked the same soul-searching questions. Historians have 'picked' at it. Military logistical analysts have 'chewed' it over warranting its merits and justification.

It simply happened because Passchendaele stood in the way of the British Forces' advance across the low country to capture from the Germans the ports of Ostend, Zeebrugge and Antwerp. This intent if successful would have eradicated the German U-Boat menace which at the time was having a devastating effect on Allied shipping.

The success of these German naval actions had in fact brought Britain to the precipice of severe rationing and in some cases mild starvation in deprived areas.

If these submarine bases could be captured then this ultimate threat would be extinguished, it would also serve to drive the German land forces back into their homeland.

Naturally the Germans were well aware of their enemies' intent and that intention must be stemmed and totally blocked.

The place, of course – Passchendaele.

This small Belgian village, whose only previous action had been the annual autumnal harvest, was now finding itself at that time of the year completely besieged on all sides by two of the greatest armies ever gathered by man, hell bent and totally committed to the infliction and unconditional devastation... all for the benefit of humanity. And all because this village held a commanding view of the salient of and around Ypres from its three hundred feet above sea level, which was extremely commanding in that part of Belgium.

When the final capitulation took place numerous reflections and 'post campaign' comments made as to its cost in human life were submitted from many quarters.

The 'cost' of human endeavour was unreservedly due to the

enormous 'bungling' and adverse decisions made entirely by people attempting to fight a war by 'antiquated inbred methods'.

Famous people would in time, lend their names to support the courage of their convictions in criticism of this battle. One in particular was Sir Edward Beddington-Behrens, who in 1967 said of it:

> 'Only British valour made up for the incompetence of our cavalry generals. Because all this happened so long ago we should not gloss over the failures of the then existing establishment. The useless sacrifice is remembered by all those still living who took part in the actual fighting.'

Another cryptic analysis came from one who himself was a fighting officer, he said:

> 'In retrospect it is amazing to me as a survivor that the infantry stuck the protracted horror of Passchendaele as bravely as they did. Every cardinal error in their handling was committed.'

And so they go on, and will continue to for generations to come. Theories for and against will attempt in a 'post-mortemistic' way to judge the horror of 1917 at Passchendaele.

Perhaps the most touching and moving statement to have arisen from this carnage was made in the aftermath of the battle. Standing on the crest of the newly taken ridge surveying what had been for three months the battlefield, a high ranking general looking over the desolation, tears running down his cheeks, emotionally drained, was heard to have coined the immortal phrase:

'Did we really send our men into this?'

Not being an historian but more of a reader and student of this 1917 conflict, and also a visitor if only occasionally to the 'site', I have attempted to state, simply by my observations based on what I have seen and read, my own personal view. The in-depth thesis on Passchendaele I will leave to the experts.

Julian Nicholls

The Battle of Passchendaele

The concept of taking Passchendaele Ridge was hatched entirely from the success achieved on Messines Ridge. Haig himself, obviously flushed with this action, could not or would not consider what immense a cost it would be if Passchendaele were to be taken for these were the times when battles had become those of attrition.

The opening rounds of the contest commenced on 16th July. There was no shadow boxing or feeling out the strength of your opponents. It was begun with an awesome 'softening up' barrage on the front between Dixmude and Bailleul. This saturation type bombardment had become the 'norm' prior to a major offensive, this fact was acknowledged by both sides.

During the period of this constant pounding the British and their allies were strengthening and consolidating all positions in anticipation of the forthcoming attack.

Many of these brave men were all too aware of the hopelessness a frontal attack would be against what they knew would be a system of strategically placed German gun emplacements which belched instant death at so many rounds per minute. As they sat before the battle writing letters to their loved ones many would have pondered on the thought that these would be the last letters they would write.

It is both difficult and testing to one's imagination to picture these troops squatting in the squalid filth of trench or shell hole, desperately compounding a letter of love and affection to those at home whilst overhead thousands of tons of death were being showered on one's fellow man.

Little fragments of Flanders mud often splattered the writing paper, to dry slowly in transportation and to end ironically in dust on the floor of many a parlour or living room in English homes when opened.

This constant bombardment lasted a very long time. At dawn on 31st July and moving along a very wide front between Boesinghe and the Comines Canal, the British Fifth Army supported by the French to the north, moved quickly and silently towards the German positions. This was the opening phase of what was to be the most infamous battle of all time.

As a result of intensive forward logistical planning the British Fifth Army were, as Haig mused, 'well positioned' for what was to take place.

Along the north flank the guards were being aided by the French. They were ordered to attack the front facing Pilkem Ridge at a point approximately named Artillery Wood.

These orders were to be implemented at first light, which on the day was approximately 4.30 a.m.

The neighbouring support regiments to the right were to follow immediately afterwards. These in fact were the Welsh 38th.

To the right of them and forming the centre of this particular point of the line stood the strength of the 51st Highland Division. Plunging forward in the vanguard were of course the battle hardy 4th Gordon Highlanders.

All the time waiting on the Ypres side of the canal as part of

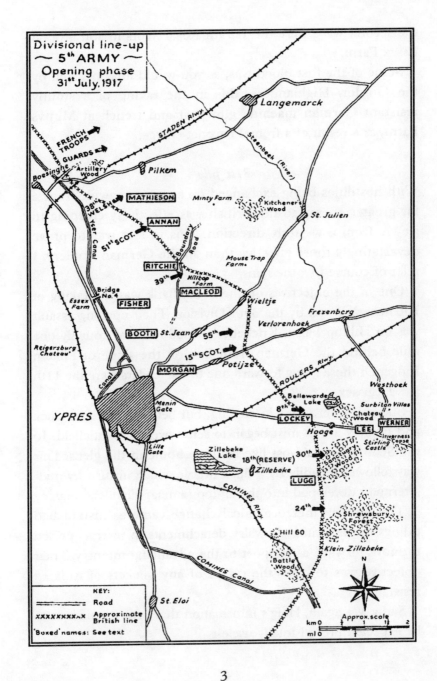

Divisional line-up
~ 5th ARMY ~
Opening phase
31st July, 1917

Langemarck

STADEN Rlwy.

Steenbeek (River)

FRENCH TROOPS
GUARDS

Boesinghe
Artillery Wood
Pilkem

MATHIESON

Minty Farm
Kitchener's Wood
St. Julien

38th WELSH

Yser Canal

ANNAN

51st SCOT.

Boundary Road

Mouse Trap Farm

RITCHIE

39th

Hilltop Farm

MACLEOD

Wieltje

Frezenberg

Bridge No. 4

Essex Farm

FISHER

Verlorenhoek

BOOTH
St. Jean
55th

Reigersburg Chateau

15th SCOT.

Potijze

ROULERS Rlwy.

Westhoek

MORGAN

Canal

Bellewarde Lake

Surbiton Villas

Menin Gate

8th

Chateau Wood

YPRES

LOCKEY

LEE

WERNER

Hooge

Inverness Copse

Lille Gate

Stirling Castle

Zillebeke Lake

18th (RESERVE)

30th

Zillebeke

LUGG

24th

Shrewsbury Forest

COMINES Rlwy.

Hill 60

Klein Zillebeke

Battle Wood

COMINES Canal

N

St. Eloi

KEY:
———————— Road
xxxxxxxxxx Approximate British line
'Boxed' names: See text

Approx. scale
km 0   1   1   2
ml 0   1   1

3

the second wave were the 1st/9th Royal Scots in and around Essex Farm.

Some of the first blood was, as you would imagine, spilt by the Gordon Highlanders, this in the taking of a stoutly resistant German machine gun post and trench at Mintys Farm, as a result of a frontal bayonet charge.

31st July

With hostilities being exchanged on a now very wide front a far greater enemy to the British was effectively creeping in slowly from a westerly direction. This in fact was to prove devastatingly more effective than all the German artillery. I refer of course to... the rains.

One of the objectives on the north flank was the taking of Kitchener's Wood by the 39th Division. Their opening assault was on Hilltop Farm. Kitchener's Wood itself lay roughly one mile behind the German front line on the slope of Pilkem Ridge. Of those going forward one of the leaders were the 11th Royal Sussex.

Successes were slow in coming, but between eleven o'clock and midday a thin mist began to settle over the battlefield. To the Scots it was almost like being at home in the glens. This was followed steadily by a thick drizzle which in turn by mid-afternoon developed into the all too familiar Flanders deluge.

This sudden meteorological change came as instant bad tidings to the awaiting cavalry detachments in reserve, poised to move forward as support to the advancing infantry. Their objective was to clear the ridges of any pockets of isolated resistance.

Sadly, yet again, Haig's information that firm terrain was to be expected proved totally useless.

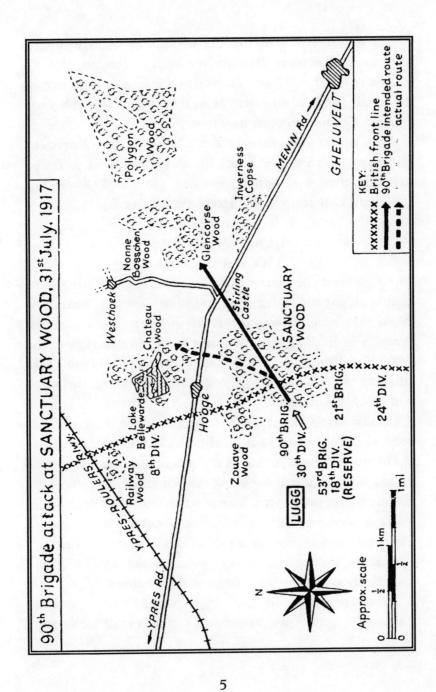

90th Brigade attack at SANCTUARY WOOD, 31st July. 1917

Polygon Wood

Nonne Bosschen Wood

Westhoek

Chateau Wood

Lake Bellewarde

Railway Wood

YPRES-ROULERS Rlwy.

8th DIV.

Zouave Wood

Hooge

Glencorse Wood

Inverness Copse

MENIN Rd

GHELUVELT

Stirling Castle

SANCTUARY WOOD

90th BRIG.

30th DIV.

LUGG

53rd BRIG.
18th DIV.
(RESERVE)

21st BRIG.

24th DIV.

YPRES Rd.

N

Approx. scale

0   ½   1km

0   ½   1ml

KEY:
xxxxxx British front line
━━━▶ 90th Brigade intended route
╌╌╌▶ actual route

5

The deterioration in weather conditions quickly slowed progress and certain detachments became 'bogged down', unable to advance. Under little or no protection and often in the open spaces of no man's land, they discovered with what ease the German gunners now found them.

A particular detachment of the Hertfordshire Regiment (600 men) who attacked on the front near St Julien now found that less than a hundred remained unscathed. Sadly but effectively, at that point the 'Herts' ceased to exist.

31st July (Middle Sector)
15th and 5th Scots

Their second objective was the Frezenburg Ridge. In contemplating the taking of this position what was failed to be taken into account was the strength of the stout German defences at Beck House and Borry Farm. Also slightly to the south the 10th and 11th Battalions of the Highland Light Infantry were facing tough opposition in taking the small hamlet of Verlorenhoek.

Finally, after some of the fiercest fighting yet, the 15th Scots secured the objectives of Beck House and Borry Farm.

Due to the superhuman efforts of this endeavour it became all too obvious that in so doing the 8th and 55ths, who were slightly to the south, were now positioned to their rear and as a result were not able to advance parallel. The 15th now offered no support on either side of this runaway advance.

Finding themselves in this position the 15th Division unenviably were now being fired on from behind.

This prospect would have been avoided had the cavalry been brought into play as support to the rear of the forward attack.

8th Division

The sector of the front line in which the 8th were to advance was, basically, the frontal centre of the whole offensive. Located north of the Menin Road but slightly to the east of what remained of the village of Hooge, they were to capture all the ground in and around Bellewarde Lake.

Hooge itself had been the nearest point the Germans had reached in their advance to Ypres itself. This is the sector in which tanks were used, most of which had been given nicknames. One in particular which was named 'Iron Rations' sadly took a direct hit near Hooge itself.

Of the 120 or so tanks in this battle only 50% reached their objectives.

30th and 8th Divisions *(continued)*

In the extremely open position on the Menin Road aptly named Clapham Junction, their advancement was checked by intensive machine gunning from the German positions in Glencourse Wood and Inverness Copse.

In particular the 6th Royal Berkshires, thinking the day won, cheerfully advanced into a relentless fusillade, totally oblivious of the error that was theirs.

The advance was now being checked and before any further progress would be made communications between the flanks must be restored and all positions relocated.

With this reforming completed further progress forward was in short bursts. In places from one shell-hole to another under the constant vigilance of the redoubtable enemy pill boxes spewed forth venom of terrible rapidity.

At nine o' clock the Menin Road was eventually traversed, this being done by a Company of the Suffolk Regiment.

When consolidation of all gained ground had been achieved the troops now waited in anticipation of an expected German counter attack. Fortunately this possibility was well defined, resulting in any possible move by the enemy being repelled by the strength and accuracy of the supporting artillery.

31st July

30th Division

The route to be taken by the 30th Division was one of a diagonal nature on a south-west to north-east angle.

From Sanctuary Wood the 21st Brigade of four battalions were to move simultaneously across the Menin Road at Stirling Castle. The objective was to capture and hold Glencourse Wood and Inverness Copse.

The sloping ground to Glencourse Wood was familiarly referred to as Surbiton Villas, slightly to the left of Clapham Junction.

It was generally accepted that the taking of this open stretch of land would prove costly and, no doubt, ingrained in the minds of these men going forward was the thought that to many it would be the last forward move they would accomplish in their lifetime.

With this in mind a reserve division in the form of the 18th was to advance forward up and through the 30th immediately Glencourse Wood had been cleared and securely held. This achieved, it was then that the final aspect would be implemented... the taking of Polygon Wood.

Unknown to all the pre-planning at Headquarters these woods were thickly defended and totally impassable. The Germans had placed crack troops in the defence of these woods. Soon it would be realised by the advancing British as they moved towards Zonnebeke that, step by step, the German opposition became progressively difficult to break. This in itself resulted in some of the most vicious hand to hand confrontations of the entire battle.

By way of accident the 53rd Brigade of the 18th Division whilst under constant fire strayed towards the wrong woods, thus finding themselves ensnared by unrelenting German machine gun fire.

A tragedy of similar magnitude fell upon a battalion of the 90th Brigade who also strayed erringly into heavy fire entering Glencourse Wood.

But the most costly punishment to be inflicted fell upon four battalions of the 18th Division, who, whilst bursting through what they considered to be a well cleared Sanctuary Wood, walked straight into the teeth of the second German defence line.

At this stage of the advancement to Passchendaele all objectives had been achieved, but at what cost? With this foremost in mind, it begged one to question the reasoning behind the planning.

The added obstacle that the extreme weather posed had played a major role in making the transition of this open ground at times, totally unnegotiable. What had once upon a time been green fertile land was now transformed into a sea of mud, pot-marked by shell cratered water holes into which many a brave wounded combatant had slid into helplessly on the saddest of routes to his maker.

This is where it is said grown mature men wept at the misery and pain they were witnessing endlessly.

Sadly, the worst was yet to come.

What had made these men weep bore no comparison to what the remaining weeks to Passchendaele held in store.

The future misery that warfare beheld would not only make men weep... in some cases it would break their hearts.

22nd August

After a period of comparatively kind weather it was decided to continue the eastward advancement. This decision was reached in light of the consolidating and regrouping which had hastily been achieved.

On the 10th August a forward thrusting operation began with three infantry divisions advancing up the gradual sloping ground known as Westhoek Ridge. Swift successes were followed by the capture of the hamlet itself.

However, although achieving success at this strong point any future advances would be withheld in order to assess the strength and tactical capacity of the German defences in and around Glencourse Wood, because this formidable obstacle now lay directly in the path of the British advance.

Pursuing the usual deliberations the initial assault on the woods was made by the London Rifle Brigade, bravely handling the expected heavy losses. They in fact overran the pillbox defences, the success to a great extent being achieved through precision hand bombing.

Following directly in the rear came the Queen's Westminsters ably supported by the London Fusiliers whose task it was to execute the 'clearing up' process in the taking of prisoners.

By mid-morning sections of the 56th Division finally cleared Glencourse Wood after what had been a truly brutal onslaught. The cost in human terms had been absolutely appalling.

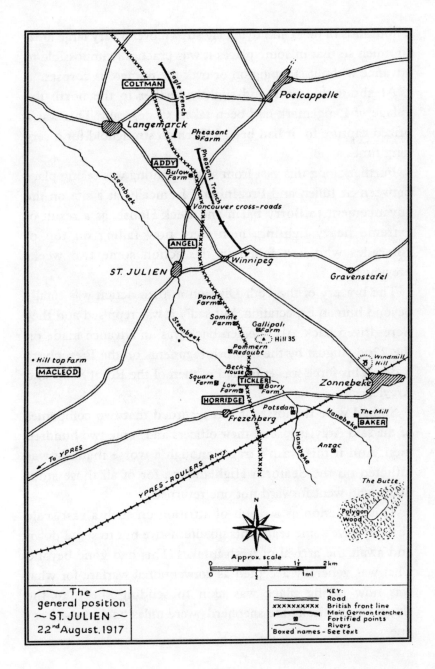

COLTMAN

Eagle Trench

Poelcappelle

Langemarck

Pheasant
Farm

ADDY

Pheasant Trench

Bulow
Farm

Steenbeek

Vancouver cross-roads

ANGEL

Winnipeg

ST. JULIEN

Gravenstafel

Pond
Farm

Steenbeek

Somme
Farm

Gallipoli
Farm

• Hill 35

Pommern
Redoubt

• Hill top farm
MACLEOD

Beck
House

Windmill
Hill

Square
Farm

TICKLER

Low
Farm

Barry
Farm

Zonnebeke

HORRIDGE

Potsdam

Hanebeke

The Mill
BAKER

Frezenberg

Hanebeke

Anzac

← To YPRES

YPRES – ROULERS Rlwy.

The Butte

Polygon
Wood

N

Approx. scale

0   1½   2 km
0   1 ml

~ The ~
general position
~ ST. JULIEN ~
22nd August, 1917

KEY:
Road
xxxxxxxxxx   British front line
Main German trenches
Fortified points
Rivers
'Boxed' names – See text

11

Thousands of dead and dying lay strewn over a very large area, so much so that in some places it was practically impossible to advance without stepping on or over the numerous corpses.

At about this time and slightly further to the north the village of Langemark had been taken strategically. This was a prized capture for it had been a German stronghold for a very long time.

Further along this vast front severe fighting was taking place between St Julien and Frezenburg. Ironically, at a site on the advancement to Borry Farm and Beck House, as a result of extreme heavy fighting, men were now falling on top of comrades who had fallen in the action some two weeks previously.

The bravery of the 16th Division in their action was totally beyond human expectation, but sadly it was repulsed and they were driven back. Also beaten back was an advance made on the 22nd August by the Scottish regiments on the Frezenburg Ridge. This force was compiled of men of the Royal Scots and Argyles.

So bad were the losses it was recorded that two companies of the said Argyles lost all their officers and some two hundred men. And if this wasn't tragic enough a worse mauling was inflicted on the Seaforth Highlanders, for of all those stout Scots who went forward not one returned.

This depletion as a result of attrition on such a vast scale virtually gave some regiments no alternative but to stand down and await the arrival of fresh intakes. This had gone beyond what was generally accepted as conventional warfare for what was now taking place was akin to sending sheep to the slaughter, ironically the shepherds were miles behind the front line.

20th September

The Push

Moving on well into September the next objective on this now very slow advancement to Passchendaele was the village of Zonnebeke. Actually little was left standing for it now held the sad distinction of having become the most heavily bombed village in Flanders.

The responsibility lay with the British Third Division. Their task held the added inducement of knowing that the newly arrived Australian troops were securely perched on the Westhoek Ridge primed to advance across the small valley of the Nannebeke. On their left lay the flattened Zonnebeke and on their right flank lay Polygon Wood.

Beyond all expectations the forward advance was made both speedily and successfully.

What was in fact remaining of the once heavily defended Glencourse Wood and Inverness Copse was now safely held. This would serve as the final stepping stone in the capitulation of the German residents on Passchendaele Ridge.

At this juncture in the proceedings the British forces stood directly north to south. On the 23rd to 24th September the strongly defended position of Eagle Trench was finally taken. This was indeed extremely valuable ground, lying as it did in a position to the north of Langemark. It had proved a serious obstacle for a long time. Well dug in and superbly defended it took great endeavour to capture this strongpoint.

Very sad to note is the fact that at this period in the campaign some 90,000 troops had been killed.

Advances made, goals reached! ...yet again... at what cost?

Yet to come was to be the most costly period in terms of

13

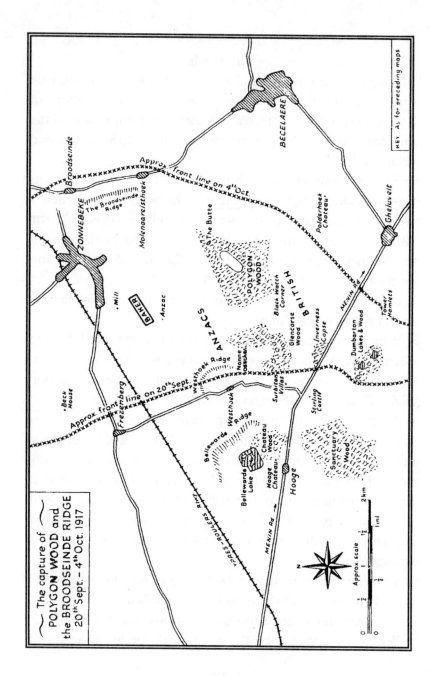

~ The capture of ~
POLYGON WOOD and
the BROODSEINDE RIDGE
20th Sept. – 4th Oct. 1917

KEY As for preceding maps

BECELAERE

Approx front line on 4th Oct.

Broodseinde

The Broodseinde Ridge

Molenaarelsthoek

ZONNEBEKE

Poelcappelle Chateau

Ghéluvelt

The Butte

POLYGON WOOD

Tower Hamlets

.Mill

BAKER

.Anzac

Black Watch Corner

MENIN Rd.

BRITISH

ANZACS

Westhoek Ridge

Nonne Bosschen

Glencorse Wood

Inverness Copse

Dumbarton Lakes & Wood

.Beck House

Approx front line on 20th Sept.

Frezenberg

Surbiton Villas

Sterling Castle

Bellewarde Ridge

Westhoek Ridge

Sanctuary Wood

Chateau Wood

YPRES–ROULERS RLWY.

Bellewarde Lake

Hooge Chateau

Hooge

MENIN Rd.

N

Approx scale

1 ½ 0 1 2 km
1 ½ 0 1 ml

14

manpower. All this was made almost sacrificially in order to clear the Passchendaele Ridge.

30th October

The final push to Passchendaele commenced at 5.30 in the morning. The Canadians in the van of the attack had orders to move forward rapidly to take the village, thus clearing a way for the following troops.

The German barrage was only slight and the Canadians made full use of this fact as they progressed to the outskirts of the village skirting both sides of what is now the main highway. This was achieved by the 12th Brigade (Brigadier-General Macbrian) consisting of the 85th Nova Scotians and the 72nd Canadian Seaforths.

Positions that had been lost in previous engagements were very hastily regained.

During the afternoon the regrouping Germans made a series of fierce counter attacks to the north, clinging desperately to lost ground, but all these attacks were successfully contained. Fierce German resistance was met on the left flank by the 58th and 63rd Divisions of the XVIII Corps.

Advancing up the muddy slopes of the Lekkerboterbeek the 63rds found themselves engulfed in knee-deep mud. This proved to be a disaster, totally disabling them from following the cover of the planned barrage.

Stuck in no-man's-land they instantly became the prime targets of not only the German infantry but also the machine gunners who had what can only be described as a field day, cutting down at random these men unable to move forward. This alone accounted for nearly a thousand casualties of which the (28th London's) Artists Rifles suffered tragic losses.

'They fell like wilting flowers before the unrelenting wind'.

31st October

Out of sheer desperation the Germans flung all of their resources into numerous counter attacks but were driven back by troops who were now consolidated in hard won positions that were unlikely to be offered so easily before the total capitulation of German mastery in and around Passchendaele.

Logistical changes took place on this day in as much as General Plumer took control of the XVIII Corps and troops from the Fifth Army, resulting in all future operations coming under the directions of one command. General Gough would still command the XIV Corps. The only other change was the relieving of Lieutenant-General Maxse (XVIII Corps) by Lieutenant-General Claud Jacob.

The next few days were busily spent in consolidating the newly gained ground with forward gun emplacements as support for what was to be the final nail in the German coffin.

During this lull in hostilities the Canadians carried out divisional reliefs, the 2nd for the 4th and the 1st for the 3rd.

This in itself would prove to have a far reaching effect in the success of the ultimate push.

4th October

Broodeseinde

This was to be recorded as the 'blackest day' of the whole war for Germany.

Extensive plans had been laid beforehand for this to be the

final thrust in order to achieve the capture and total dominance of the Passchendaele Ridge.

Both sides were well aware of the existence of this 'make or break' operation. It was assumed that the Germans were not fully aware of when this was to happen but on the day this was to prove debatable.

On the night of the 3rd, under a shrouded full moon, column after column, thousands of men, moved up to their jumping off point for the attack which was due to commence at 0600 hours.

The element of surprise seems to have been sacrificed when, at 0515, intense German shelling rained down on the advancing British and Commonwealth lines, the brunt borne by the Anzac troops.

Although grouping in close formation to minimise losses it was sad to note that losses were to prove inevitable. As a result of this unexpected bombardment many died without ever firing a shot in defence.

At 6 a.m. what only can be described as 'all hell' broke loose the full length of the German line as a pulverising barrage fell unrelentingly upon the enemy. Already having lost one man in seven from the German barrage the Anzacs rose from the mud, ghostly in the mist and drizzle of this October dawn. Some moved forward with lighted cigarettes all aglow, stoutly in formation this time, determined to win the prize ahead for their comrades who only seconds earlier had laid down their lives beside them. In their thousands they 'oozed' forward, blinded by this determination and totally oblivious of what was being thrown at them.

The attacking formation consisted thus: to the left flank stood the 11th and 48th British, in the centre lay the entire

17

strength of the Australian and New Zealand contingents (the 1st, 2nd and 3rd Anzacs) and to their right was the 5th, 7th and 21st British and of course the Canadians.

Surprisingly swift advances were made through the mud which had been caused by the rain draining from the targeted ridge. By mid morning the 24th Battalion of the Australians had now secured a position on the ridge. The cost in human terms had been disastrous, almost fifty per cent had fallen in this onslaught. To the left of the Australians and along this front before Passchendaele the New Zealanders were advancing over Abraham Heights, a short distance from what has become the largest cemetery in Belgium – Tyne Cot.

They were now firmly secured on the Gravenstafel Ridge a mere breath away from a foothold on the slight ahead, which would then give them an overlooking view of the ultimate objective... the remains of Passchendaele itself.

By twelve noon every planned objective had been captured, with thousands of surrendering Germans now in captivity. Looking around, little ground was left that was not covered by the dead of both sides, serving once and for all as a memorial to the futility of modern day warfare. For never had any previous conflict taken such a heavy toll on human life.

With everything somewhat secured and sweeping up operations taking place it was felt in some quarters that a further advance was necessary, but this decision was put on hold. The immediate need was to re-group and hold firm in light of a possible counter attack. For it was known that the Germans had a reserve strength of eight divisions in close order and beyond that a further six of fresh troops waiting in the nearby Belgian hinterland.

What wasn't known by the Allies was the fact that the German munitions were now almost exhausted.

At 2.00 p.m. General Sir Herbert Plumer (2nd Army) reviewed the gains that had been made and then decided at that point that no further advancement would be made. He had, however, at around 11 o' clock considered his options when he felt it necessary to capitalise on the Anzacs' morning success. This also seemed feasible to General Godley (II Anzacs) but it was felt by General Birdwood that a further push should not take place until the artillery had been re-positioned and also the chain of communications been consolidated.

Another given to further advancement was Lieutenant-General Morland (X Corps) who personally felt that a push north opposite the southern flank of the Germans who lay directly facing the 1st Anzacs might at that particular stage achieve greater things.

Major-General Shoubridge (7th Division) was quick to point out that a possible gamble of this nature was uncertain because at that particular time no commanders were totally knowledgeable of the devastating cost this advance forward had taken.

So Plumer's decision called a cessation to the day's hostilities in view of the possible German counter attack.

The demoralisation of the German troops was almost complete. As an example, in opposing the thrust of the Anzacs, the 45th German Reserve Division had lost 83 officers and 2,800 other ranks (this does not include the wounded) and the 4th German Guard Division, 86 officers and 2,700 others.

Ludendorf, whose plan it was originally, said afterwards:

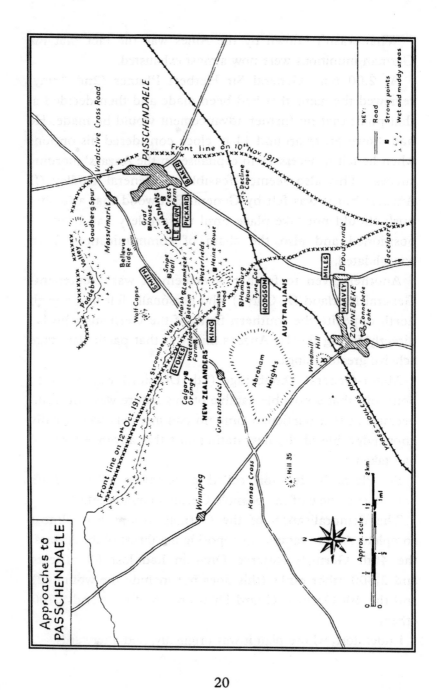

Approaches to PASSCHENDAELE

PASSCHENDAELE

Front line on 10th Nov 1917

Vindictive Cross Road

Goudberg Spur

Masselmarkt

Bellevue Ridge

Paddebeek Valley

Wolf Copse

Graf House

Crest Farm

BAKER

PICKARD

LE BLUN

CANADIANS

Snipe Hall

Waterfields

Heine House

Stroombeek

Marsh Bottom

SMITH

Decline Copse

Hamburg House

Tyne Cot

HODGSON

Broodseinde

Becelaere

MILES

HARVEY

ZONNEBEKE

Zonnebeke Lake

AUSTRALIANS

Augustus Wood

KING

Waterloo Farm

STOKES

Calgary Grange

Gravenstafel

NEW ZEALANDERS

Abraham Heights

Windmill Hill

Front line on 12th Oct 1917

Stroombeck Valley

Winnipeg

Kansas Cross

Hill 35

YPRES–ROULERS Rly

N

Approx scale

2 km
1 ml

KEY:
Road
Strong points
Wet and muddy areas

'The battle was extraordinarily severe' with enormous losses and the idea of holding the line more densely failed to be the remedy. The Germans were not alone in suffering terrible casualties. The 1st and 2nd Anzacs, who in turn were opposed by two German divisions consisting of the 10th (Ersatz) and 6th Bavarians with the 187th in reserve, suffered the following casualties – 392 officers and 7,683 other ranks. That in itself was only one aspect of the entire battle.

The victorious who survived the battle and who now gazed from this war-scarred ridge beyond into Belgium, saw the greenery untouched by the savagery and death belching of the artillery and mortar fire, a rich fertile soil which would become a final resting place to German and Commonwealth young alike never to see their homelands again. Their emotions were epitomised by one great poet who wrote:

'You must come over and join us, we are having a wonderful time – dying.'

Finally

The hour won... the day gained... the final objective achieved... but at what cost?

For on that day the climax had taken place of the most futile of military engagements in the annals of modern history.

The final capture and holding of the high ground in and around Passchendaele had been achieved by the expertise and relentless determination of the four Canadian divisions.

In years to come German General Ludendorf, whilst writing his memoirs, remarked of the Canadian onslaught thus:

'They charged like a bull against the iron wall which kept them from the submarine basis.'

Further substantial ground was gained on 10th November

21

but the battle for Passchendaele was finally over, for this had been achieved four days earlier on 6th November.

On 8th November General Plumer placed the command of the Second Army in the hands of Sir Henry Rawlinson.

Plumer himself left the very next day to take up command of the British Army in Italy.

Total Casualties of the Canadian Corps at Passchendaele
(26th October – 11th November)

	Officers		Other Ranks	
	Killed	Wounded	Killed	Wounded
1st Canadian Div.	42	63	871	1746
2nd Canadian Div.	34	71	924	1715
3rd Canadian Div.	58	88	1174	1964
4th Canadian Div.	36	70	792	1679
Other Canadian Troops	6	9	94	298
	176	301	3855	7402

The cost to the Germans was staggering. A total of 73 Divisions had taken part during the period 15th July to 10th November.

The German Fourth Army alone recorded casualties totalling 217,000 men, of which 35,000 were known killed with 48,000 missing, presumed dead.

The End

The Menin Road –
Ypres to Gheluvelt

The Menin Gate

This illustration views this vast memorial from the eastern end. Through the arch can clearly be seen the main tower of the Cloth Hall in Ypres main square. Carved on its walls are the names of 54,000 dead who have no known grave 'known only unto God'. During the First World War this entrance was guarded by two stone lions which, after the conflict, were presented to the Australian people. They now stand proudly outside the Parliamentary Building in Canberra.

I was surprised and yet somewhat proud to find a small number of Nicholls engraved on this great epitaph and I wondered if they were Cornish relatives from the past who had left their native shores to seek fame and fortune in Australia when the tin mining industry collapsed in the 1800s.

The Cloth Hall

Whenever one sees this magnificent structure it is so difficult to accept that it rose like a phoenix out of the ashes, being completely rebuilt from rubble after 1918. How proud and defiant it must have appeared to the invading Germans yet again in 1939.

Today it houses perhaps the finest of First World War museums in its vast first floor hall. Significantly wherever you care to wander in and around the immediate confines of Ypres it is so difficult to lose sight of what has become so symbolic of the city and its people.

'They came, they saw, but could not conquer.'

The Main Square, Ypres

This is the other side of the Cloth Hall. This spacious square as if protected by the overlooking Cloth Hall became known to soldiers from all over the world and became the focal point of mustering of units en route to the front line in the push to capture Passchendaele.

So bad was the continuous pounding the historic square suffered, it is said by many that even the rats left Ypres.

Nowadays it houses the main shops and a weekly market plus bus stops to many outlying districts. On a fine evening there is nowhere better to enjoy the many outside cafeterias of the square, sipping a local beer and savouring the hospitality.

The Ramparts Cemetery

Walking south along the fortress wall from the Menin Gate you could be excused for missing this little cemetery set amongst the trees overlooking the moat and the other main entrance to the city, the Lille Gate. A pleasant time to visit this spot is at sunset when, on a particularly quiet evening you can close your eyes and listen to the ghostly troop movements.

Ypres Reservoir Cemetery

A short walk from the Cloth Hall and near to the local prison lies this well kept cemetery of rectangular shape which I visited very early in the morning. It must qualify as being the closest cemetery to the British War Graves Commission whose headquarters are in nearby Elangstraat – a place I heartily recommend to those in search of burial sites.

Brigadier Frank Maxwell

This is the grave of Brigadier General Frank Maxwell, one of the most highly decorated and ranked officers to have lost his life in World War I. He won the Victoria Cross whilst serving with the 18th Lancers in India. Whilst commanding the 27th Infantry Brigade his headquarters suffered a direct hit killing him and many of his fellow officers – he was 46 years old.

On his headstone are the following words:

'A perfect gentleman, loved by his men and adored by his family.'

Hellfire Corner

In this illustration a lorry waits to cross the Menin Road from the direction of Potijze towards Zillebeke. One cannot imagine today how hostile these crossroads were. It was the main thoroughfare of all troop movements along the Menin Road and adjacent areas. Although at times camouflaged by canvas screens it was well within sight and range of the German artillery positioned on the elevated ground to the east. So many troops lost their lives that it was decided to restrict all major movements of men to and from the front line to be implemented at night time.

The detection of the slightest movement on the part of our troops would result in a severe pounding from the Germans, with devastating effect. Our troops would then seek refuge in places with names like Cork Cottage, Rifle Farm and Boundary Farm, hence the name The Corner of Fire in Hell.

The Menin Road Cemetery

This is the first cemetery one comes across when commencing the walk along the Menin Road towards Gheluvelt, a short distance from the centre of Ypres. Looking east from this place one can clearly define the gradual slope of the Menin Road into the position of the German guns.

Birr Crossroads Cemetery

This small cemetery lies approximately one kilometre from Hellfire Corner and no doubt houses the remains of many killed in and around Hellfire Corner. It was here that I stopped for a short break on my walk from Ypres along the Menin Road to Gheluvelt.

'A place of peace and thought.'

Hooge Crater Cemetery

The cemetery can be seen from a distance of half a kilometre. I wandered off the main Menin Road to try to visualise the battlefield between Hooge and Sanctuary Wood. It is there that this photograph was taken. What is now a cornfield was once the place where thousands died trying to take the distant high ground. I later returned to the main road in order to continue my walk.

The Menin Road at Hooge

It is here that I stopped at the village of Hooge which was totally flattened during the battles and was only fought for because of its value as slightly elevated ground. Looking back towards Hellfire Corner it is easy to see the ground rising gradually on the straight run up towards Clapham Junction, another site of vast hostility.

Hooge Cemetery

In this beautifully cared for cemetery I sat and took this photograph from what had been German positions.

Looking down the slope they would have seen the advancing British Troops. It also serves as a reminder that our troops were always advancing upwards because of the Germans' superior position of the high ground in the Ypres salient. In the distance is Sanctuary Wood. It is also noticeable that even today there is still a shortage of trees on this battlefield of nearly eighty years ago.

Glencourse Wood

Having wandered slightly to the left near Clapham Junction, I was keen to acquire a glimpse of Glencourse Wood.

This was the scene of many terrible skirmishes, most of which were hand to hand in order to destroy the German machine gun positions which held total superiority over the surrounding countryside.

So important was the position of this woodland that it changed hands on many occasions. In fact it is ironic to think that so many brave soldiers on both sides died, simply for possession of some trees.

Clapham Junction (Menin Road)

As one can see this is where the straight Menin Road from Ypres makes a slight right hand turn before continuing straight again towards Gheluvelt. This was also the sight of bloody action in nearby Groves such as Inverness Copse, Dumbarton Wood, Stirling Castle – as you will see by the names a great deal of Scottish troops were concentrated. The white estate car is coming from the direction of Glencourse Wood, the road I had wandered along in the previous illustration.

Today it is just another fork road, almost a rural backdrop, but in 1917 it was hell itself. The surrounding graves are testament to this.

Royal Rifle Corps Memorial

On the Menin Road near Clapham Junction stands this small memorial to the Kings Royal Rifle Corps. A great deal of action was centred around here because of the close proximity to the Bellavoorde Chateau and Lake.

Many fell near this spot which is now a theme park, a fact which makes one stop years on and ponder the thought of whether it was all worth it.

As my walk now brought me nearer to Gheluvelt I came in contact with an increasing number of monuments, one of which is the above, dedicated to the officers and men of the Fifth Australian Division and their exploits amongst others in the Third Battle of Ypres (1917) at nearby Broodseinde and Polygon Wood.

Gloucestershire Memorial

This is the Gloucestershire Memorial 1.5km west of Gheluvelt. It is situated almost in the forecourt of a car showroom. It could easily be overlooked by people driving by, but stands proud as the regiment it commemorates, a regiment renowned in the British Army for its fighting qualities and integrity.

18th Division Memorial (1st)

On my walk I came at last to the 18th Division Memorial. This stands across and slightly up the road from the Monument of the Gloucesters. It stands on ground slightly elevated on what I suppose could be called the 'brow' of the hill. In the background lies Dumbarton Woods, home and shelter to many of our troops. It is also the last monument on the way.

After taking this photograph I continued the final kilometre and a half into Gheluvelt. By this time I was low on energy and had completely run out of film for my camera.

Conclusion

As I sat at the bus stop in Gheluvolt awaiting transport to Ypres I reflected that the day's walk had been well worth it. I had visited places where great battles had been fought, places which before I had only been able to imagine.

I had always felt that I would one day traverse these fields of blood along the Menin Road, trying desperately to picture what had really taken place and simply by my mere presence being able to stop and think of all those young men who never returned from here.

As we approached Ypres by bus I couldn't help but think that in 1917 we would have been urging the driver to greater deeds, fearing the Germans might detect our presence near Hellfire Corner and open up on us.

Langemark to
Polygon Wood

On a grey Saturday in May I set out from Ypres. As the weather looked suspiciously threatening I decided to board the Langemark bus at Ypres railway station. I must admit to possessing an ulterior motive in the form of a pilgrimage on behalf of my family.

My destination was the village of Pilkem which lies slightly north of Ypres and a kilometre or so south west of Langemark. It was in this vicinity that some of the fiercest close combat occurred. It was also near here on what was known as Pilkem Ridge that my grandmother's brother, Ivor Rees, won the Victoria Cross for bravery. The citation appears overleaf.

I tried exceedingly hard to imagine the precise area but it was difficult after 77 years because the ground itself was so mortally wounded from constant explosions of every accountable size that the countryside was completely redesigned and husbanded by the local people after the war.

Comforting myself that somewhere near was where 'Uncle Ivor' had performed his heroic deeds, I set out on my walk which would take me almost directly south east to Zonnebeke and Tyne Cot Cemetery then on to Polygon Wood, a site of terrible bloodshed and death where I would end my walk having covered a greater part of the land featured in the battle for Passchendaele.

SERGEANT IVOR REES
11th South Wales Borderers

Full Name: Ivor Rees.

Place of Birth: Union Street, Felinfoel, Llanelli, Carmarthenshire. The family later moved to 18 Long Row, Felinfoel.

Date of Birth: 18th October, 1893.

Father: David Rees.

Mother: Ann Rees (nee Bowen).

Father's Occupation: Electrical Engineer.

Education: Pwll Llanelli Rural School.

Pre-Service Employment: Steelworker at Llanelli Steelworks.

Service Record: Enlisted South Wales Borderers, 9th November, 1914 (Service No. 20002); posted overseas 4th December, 1915; Lance Corporal, 5th August, 1915; Corporal, 1st December, 1915; Sergeant, 19th September, 1916; CSM, 5th September, 1917; returned to Britain, 11th February, 1918; discharged, 31st March, 1921; re-enlisted 4th Welsh Regiment (Territorial Force); discharged 30th December, 1921; served as CSM to the 2nd Carmarthenshire Home Guard during the Second World War.

Rewards, Decorations and Medals: Victoria Cross (for action at Pilkem, Belgium, 31st July, 1917); 1914-15 Star; British War Medal; Victory Medal; Defence Medal; Coronation Medal (1937); Coronation Medal (1953); Victory Medal (USA issue, clasps for Meuse-Argonne, Aisne-Marne, Defensive Sector). He also received an illuminated address from the villagers of Pwll, Llanelli.

Post-Service Employment: Unemployed for two years after the Great War then employed by Llanelli Borough Council as a Water Inspector and Cleansing Superintendent until his retirement in 1959.

Married: Martha, daughter of Evan and Sarah Jenkins of Llanelli (formerly of Towyn, Merioneth), 30th September, 1917.

Children: Two sons and three daughters.

Died: 11th March, 1967, at his home, 5 Craddock Street, Llanelli.

Buried: Cremated.

Memorials: None known.

Location of VC: South Wales Borderers Museum, Brecon.

Citation for VC: L.G. 14th September, 1917.

> "For most conspicuous bravery in attack. A hostile machine-gun opened fire at close range, inflicting many casualties. Leading his platoon forward by short rushes, Sergeant Rees gradually worked his way round the right flank to the rear of the gun position. When he was about twenty yards from the machine-gun he rushed forward towards the team, shot one and bayonetted another. He then bombed the large concrete emplacement killing five and capturing thirty prisoners of whom two were officers, in addition to an undamaged gun."

He was decorated with the VC by H.M. King George V at Buckingham Palace, 26th September, 1917.

The Canadian Memorial near St Julien
(The Resting Soldier)

The road from Langemark is very straight with nothing of any significance except the numerous farmhouses one passes. It is not until reaching the busy crossroads near St Julien that you encounter the first evidence that you are on what was once a battlefield. This crossing of roads was known to all in 1917 as Winnipeg and Cross, aptly named by the Canadians.

It was near this site that the Canadians bore the brunt of the first German gas attacks, a horror of man's making in creating death and misery to his fellow humans under the guise of modern warfare.

It was in this peaceful little corner of 'Canada' that I sat and had my picnic lunch on the Saturday of Whitsun 1995.

The Commemorative Plaque

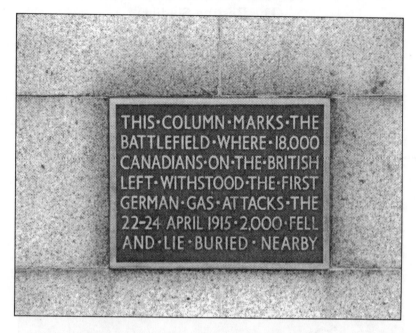

THIS·COLUMN·MARKS·THE
BATTLEFIELD·WHERE·18,000
CANADIANS·ON·THE·BRITISH
LEFT·WITHSTOOD·THE·FIRST
GERMAN·GAS·ATTACKS·THE
22-24 APRIL 1915·2,000·FELL
AND·LIE·BURIED·NEARBY

The words tell it all but cannot begin to describe the appalling suffering inflicted by these gas attacks often culminating in a slow and painful death.

The Canadians were in no way prepared, they did not have the protection of gas masks. In some cases as a last resort men would urinate on cloths and cover their faces as a minor form of antidote to this obnoxious gas that floated on a down wind, silently yet deadly across no man's land. So many suffered and died yet ironically not by gunshot wounds.

After leaving the Canadian War Memorial I decided to head due east to take in the sloping ground towards Tyne Cot Cemetery. The farmland I traversed was virtually all no man's land during the battle. The adopted names became famous during the battles for Ypres – London Ridge and Abraham Heights. No heights at all realistically speaking, only slightly higher ground than the surrounding area. It was near this site that I almost missed the above monument, slightly hidden in a set back situation near a fork in two roads.

Tyne Cot Cemetery

This picture is from a position occupied by the Canadians, previously mentioned as Abraham Heights. Where the cemetery now stands were the strong machine gun emplacements which would come to be known as 'pill boxes'. A company of Tynesiders (Infantrymen) called these positions 'Tyne Cottages' because of the similarity they bore to the cottages back home in their native 'Geordieland'. These positions were almost impregnable and were only finally captured at an amazing cost in lives because of the unprotected land the Germans controlled from these slightly elevated positions.

Tyne Cot Cemetery

This is the view of the cemetery from the eastern approach which is from the main road running all along the top of the Passchendaele Ridge from the village itself to the village of Zonnebeke. One must imagine that in the final days of the battle little or nothing remained of these villages as a result of the constant bombardments.

What is now lush farmland, as can be seen, was in 1917 little more than corpse filled potholes and lakes of 'oozing' mire where many soldiers breathed their last.

Tyne Cot Cemetery

This picture is taken from the centre of the cemetery looking towards the main entrance and interestingly across the open ground of Abraham Heights, only this time from the German's eye view. One can see from this angle the distinct advantage this sloping terrain lent to the German effort.

In the far distance can be seen the distant skyline of Ypres.

I was disappointed, for at about this time it had started to rain and did not allow me the quality of light which I otherwise would have had.

It did however serve to remind me how heavy the rainfall can be in this particular part of Belgium. On a wall at the top of the cemetery are the names of thousands 'known only unto God'.

Tyne Cot Cemetery – The Central Cross

This monument was actually built on top of one of the German pill boxes as can be seen in this picture below.

Polygon Wood

After leaving Zonnebeke I walked the short distance past what was known as the 'Glasgow Spur' en route to Polygon Wood. It was near 'Albania Wood' that I encountered this small but beautifully maintained little cemetery surrounded by a shield of well planted trees.

At about this time the sun put in a brief appearance and suddenly the world seemed better, even if in the company of the dead.

I was now approaching the wood itself. The last of the Killing Fields I would visit on this my last journey.

Polygon Wood
The Buttes Military Cemetery (The Approach)

Just off the road and through a gap in the trees one sees the obelisk that stands on a mound overlooking the 'resting' place. It is also the site where the Germans concentrated their machine gun positions making it extremely difficult for the troops attacking from the easterly direction.

Polygon Wood
The Buttes Military Cemetery

This remarkable cemetery is located in the centre of the woods and was virtually built as a result of a large rectangular stretch of land being cleared. This picture is from on top of the mound seen in the previous photograph.

To the left hand side most of the graves are in summer time emblazoned with red roses which is so touchingly symbolic.

Polygon Wood
The Buttes Cemetery

The main structure stands as if guarding the row upon row of neatly lined gravestones.

This perhaps is one of the most unique of all the cemeteries in and around Ypres.

The surrounding wood was itself held by both sides on numerous occasions... the gravestones themselves will tell you at what cost. Most of them lay where they fell.

So my journey came to its final conclusion. As I left Polygon Wood I took the road through the famous 'Sans Souci Valley' heading in the direction of the Zonnebeke-Ypres road.

After visiting 'Borry Farm', another place of fierce fighting, I returned to Ypres having satisfactorily covered a vast area of ground contested over by both sides. I was glad that I had achieved it all 'on foot' for this was the only way.

Although seventy-seven years on and aided by a stout pair of walking shoes I needed above all that extra ingredient... an acquired imagination. For without this I could never have begun to visualise what had taken place at the time, of the tens of thousands of troops of both sides concentrated into such a small area.

They came to fight from Canada, Australia, India, Africa, England, Scotland, Wales, Ireland and many other far corners of the earth, all because they were loyal to the cause.

And the cause?

A ridge of ground one hundred and fifty feet higher than the surrounding countryside – Passchendaele.

A Country Lane...1916

I sat upon a public bench
Eroding time of day
Observing of a lad and maid
That happened along that way.

Their happiness it seemed serene,
Alone, 'twas theirs to share,
In two short years that soon would pass
The war their hearts would tear.

Like all the youth who faced the truth
His country's pride to save,
This proud and honest Cornish lad
Now sleeps in unmarked grave.

When news arrived one August morn
Those left behind were gathering corn,
The village mourned for weeks to pass
None more than that poor, broken lass.

And so, at last the years have passed
But memories long remain,
Of that fine lad and his fair maid
Who walked that fragrant lane.

Yet, sometimes when in wintertime
Whilst walking through the rain
The maid, still blinded by her love
Stands waiting in the lane.

Julian Nicholls